You Cannot Chain A Phoenix

I0117871

Nigel Pearce

chipmunkapublishing
the mental health publisher

Published by
Chipmunkapublishing
United Kingdom

http://www.chipmunkapublishing.com

Copyright © Nigel Pearce 2013

ISBN   978-1-78382-031-3

Edited by Lesley Kirk

About Chipmunkapublishing

Mental health books give a voice to writers with mental illness around the world. At Chipmunkapublishing we raise awareness of mental health and the stigma surrounding mental health problems by encouraging society to listen. We are documenting mental health literature as a genre so history does not forget the survivors and carers of people with mental illness and disabilities.

Chipmunkapublishing gratefully acknowledge the support of Arts Council England.

Author Biography

Nigel was born in 1959 into a family with profound faults lines. When these cracks became chasms he runaway and lived in the 'counter-culture'. He has both interrelated mental and physical health problems which persist. However he continues to rise like a phoenix from every death-in-life and has gained a B.A (Hons) and a Diploma of Higher Education at the Open University and a Certificate in English Studies from Warwick University. At present he is studying for a Humanities degree with a specialism in creative writing. Nigel is the author of four previous titles with Chipmunkapublishing

Nigel, B.A (Hons), Dip.H.E, who is the author of four previous books published by Chipmunkapublishing and has spent the last year deeply immersed in the Western philosophical tradition. This has opened new avenues of enquire and some new solutions. The poetry reflects these influences in part but also the struggles and trumps of living with both mental and related physical illnesses. They are the poems and meditations of a Phoenix, who has been left for dead many times but he has always confounded the psychiatrists and physicians by rising resplendent and renewed when they had left him for dead. Nigel is currently pursuing a Humanities Degree in Creative Writing

Poem for Richard B' upon his premature death (Revised).

Looked in those eyes and saw a galaxy of stars like death's untameable love,

Not beloved Cohen's 'bird on a wire' but your words with syllables unstained,

Tigers glancing out of the shadows but always they would purr perfect pulses,

Asymmetry maybe but who wants to be a square, disequilibrium of pure tides,

They would wash us both away into torrents of tremendous terror but tenderly,

Always the day dawned danced its words across our minds, the cloud of light.

A scroll not rolled out for those staid sane pens with their soulless nib scratch,

Our pens etched souls of amber, but words will reverberate like love and loss.

A teenage political prisoner is detained on two psychiatric wards in 1970s.

An older monk on a secure ward also talked of Tim Leary and Che so we colluded,
The nurse without eyes just a film covered One presumed in purveyor of darker art,
A poet wrote in metaphor not grasped by those who had embalmed patients' minds,

We were born into the bell-jar of discontent but do not worry doctor has the thorium,
But the clientele spat sputum into cardboard spittoons not emptied but flung in rage,
So we were hidden on wards with sycophants, faces like brick and mortar monotone,

A nurse wanted patients to be aborted cherubs of heaven, some were like banshees,
No one commented until the ritual burial of a demon because things are hot in a hell,
Just play bingo pleads Janus therapist while he winks towards some wincing nurses,

No take over the asylum and make it your campus howls that interned revolutionary,
The patients rise-up like tigers but then the panzer squad prepare a chemical Cosh,
As electro-convulsive therapy was had by all in the aftermath, the wires just buzzed,

Not forgotten were those whose deaths in the catacombs which left us a bitter taste,
Bitter is the taste of lemon, lemon is yellow that will colour us if cancer strikes in liver.

Haiku.

The winter spirit
Smiles, mistletoe whispers but
Always breaks like ice.

Haiku.
This sun shimmered stalks
Of corn pieces wounded flesh
And shed icy blood.

The Corpse.

The corpse of the ancestors lies uneasy in a sea of shimmering silver memory,
Rememorized tides which break with stern certainty on this poet's black pages,
His was born in a tremble of fear and fists he was regularly informed as a child,
Therefore poetry was a refuge from his threats and her corrosive suicidal spits,
A book and then a pen and pad were walls he built for protection from a family,
He could sniff a putrid stench of this damned and green wormed corpse home,
It overcame him and cast a spell of musing that metamophorised into dreams,
The doctors would call this insanity a madness born of a dopamine deficiency,
And who would believe the poet's scream of pain written in reams of red verse.

Corpses of family lie buried deep and are nothing now than haunting spectres,
I exorcize them not with holy rite but with a sacred sacrament of wording write.

The Disappeared and the Non-believed.

The 16 *disappeared* who were executed by a terrible beauty was born Easter 1916,
The poet does not make the moral mores of life; but weaves metaphors, analogies,
The 16 and Us in the thousands: the suicides, medication deaths and plighted lives,
We non-Believed unlike the un-believed were not just left in solitary silence to suffer,
We told our stories to psychiatrists, nurses and social workers and a terrible lie born
Called 'paranoia' with punishment for telling the truth about a family, home, hospital,
The 16 dead had a bullet in the back of the head, but the non-believed were tortured,
Electrodes put on our heads and wired up to the grid get us 'right' again ECT weekly,
Drugs rammed into us a plastic syringe death hit but by the nurses for our own good,
Therapists who built-up trust with us and then wrote reports saying we were deluded,
People were paid to care for us; it was not a few rogues but the caring system it-self,
Many patients and poets took the hard way out and with overdose or rope, staff had
Tidy formula to explain deaths, but patients knew and had talked with them it is true,
One patient-poet writes in blood the name of every suicide and death by medication,
It is his blood and names written on golden scroll will be read at the time of nemesis.
The 16 may or not have been informants, but we were in council care and hospitals,
Yes you have guessed there is more, this is poetry not journalism, apply imagination
We may not be believed, perpetrators were elite carers who are injury which endure.

Spring 2013.

Spring aches in their heart of embers, serpents do glide through Time,
The apple blossom is not impregnated artificially with resin to fall down,
Do silicone petals have the same thirst for Sun the organic one claims?
The world has transmogrified it is no longer carbon based but concrete,
Trees of luminous green Plasticine are still sensitive to the tender touch,
Whose touch, Midas touch, no gold finger is on the run from the masses.

Children gaze with eyes of Eve far too early? Know polar ice is melting,
Ice melts in a deluge and a hurricane howls today's star crossed lovers,
A revelation? Juliet was but thirteen and Friar Lawrence an apothecary,
Do the planets rotate in a different way today, tides of lovers unmoved?
Poet knows lovers will lie with the curse of the elders chiselled in stone,
The sage can hand a phial to numb the pain or the pen to write in blood.

Poem to lost love.

'An intellectual is someone whose mind watches itself.
I am happy to be both halves, the watcher and the watched.'
-Albert Camus.

The worms are in her hair and creep like crazy symmetry of slurred syllogisms,
Her black and translucent pupils are the corridor back into the infinity of inferno,
The nymphets were left broken like alabaster dolls sacrificed to a dumb phallus,
Some gathered their skirts and stole the microdots hidden in haste but now lost,
Camus stands alone a pillar of stone and utters his words of wisdom but weeps,
Back in sputnik I spin trying to keep the letters of R. D. Laing 'Knots' on a page,
Tumble into a purple zone through a rose garlanded window etched in her mind,
Put the harpsichord concertos on again please I love them much Hermes sighs,
The statue of Camus vaporized, Hermes levitated and we went weaving waves.

I write these words about those days of dreams and wish my love not died in vain,
We were children of ether who were not of this world, entombed within its bounds.

Camus and Hermes. (revised).

'An intellectual is someone whose mind watches itself.
I am happy to be both halves, the watcher and the watched.'
                                        -Albert Camus.

The worms are in her hair and creep like crazy symmetry of slurred syllogisms,
Her black and translucent pupils are the corridor back into the infinity of inferno,
The nymphs were left broken like alabaster dolls sacrificed to his dumb phallus,
Some gathered their skirts and stole the microdots hidden in haste by now lost,
A spectre is reading the words of ferial incarnations of Camus, who had arrived,
Back in the sputnik I spin and try to keep the words of Laing: 'Knots' on a page,
Tumbling into the libido Zone again next door through a rose garlanded window,
'Put Bach harpsichord concertos on again', Hermes said, I love so but too much',
Camus vaporized, Hermes levitated the trip trembled on like a weaving of tissues.

The Day I realized René Descartes was wrong.

You were an 'I' who could not pass through the eye of a needle too wealthy in ideas,
That Doubt of dream games of molten wax but you were not an explorer of Psyche,
An ideologue who would doubt all but Cogito Ergo Sum another fake along that Way,
Conjured an Evil Genius to deceive all, the thought of deception without a hesitation,
Squares become triangles in a Cartesian circle, round and round you were just dizzy,
Baseline was always going to be Saint Anselm, the proof of perfection by God alone.

René the rabbits were all in a bag the one you pulled out was Carroll's White Rabbit,
That day my doubt became an epiphany was when the lie of Cartesian Doubt died,
An awaking of a lotus flower in the moonlight, rebirth in the mists of lunacy and love.

.

Some Primary Notes.

1) 'Is personal identity a matter of bodily continuity?'

The question of personal identity is of concern to us because we are thinking self-conscious beings. There are two major divisions within philosophy generally; Physicalism and Idealism. The former are concerned with explanations which include matter rather than spirit, a material base for consciousness. The latter are inclined rather to see consciousness as independent of physical being. The debate around personal identity was begun by John Locke, he was replying in some ways to the 'received authority' of Aristotle and the doctrines of the church. However his analysis as the first of the British Empiricists was innovatory. He saw human beings as not being born with *a priori* knowledge but rather being *tabular rosa* i.e. a black sheet upon which impressions are made. Therefore, we are in a new situation with Locke in that the human identity is something we create.

For Locke there was the question of the culpability of the individual, before the Law and eschatologically. He therefore tried to establish the true nature of human identity in this context. For him, it was a 'forensic' question. He differentiated between the bodily continuity and the psychological. Calling the physical human a 'man' i.e. a physical living being who ages over time. But for Locke it was essential to establish the essential nature of human identity. For this he used the term 'person'. A person' was 'a rational thinking thing conscious of itself for itself' John Locke.

Therefore it was 'psychological rather than bodily continuity that Locke was concerned with. He used the 'thought-experiment' of 'The Prince and The Cobbler' to illustrate this as follows: The Prince wakes up in the body of the Cobbler, and the Cobbler wakes up in the body of the Prince. because for Locke personal identity is established by 'psychological identity over time' the identity of the Prince now is truly in the body of the Cobbler, but for Locke culpability is to do with psychological identity rather than bodily continuity.

This created a new 'conversation' about the nature of physical identity. Locke was answered by Thomas Reid who thought his position could not be held logically. Reid used the 'thought experiment' of the young boy and the Calvary officer as follows: a young boy steals an apple from tree, then as a young man is distinguished in battle, but as a mature General cannot remember the act of the child. Now for Locke he would not have been culpable but /Reid saying this is illogical because it denies the 'transitive relation' of: A=B, B=C and therefore A=C. thus for Reid there is continuity of psychological memory with a material base i.e. the 'Calvary officer'

David Hume would answer them both saying that true to Empiricism we should stay rooted a *posterori* experience. So he looked d to his experiences and 'introspected' and found that there nothing but a series of actors crossing the stage of life. We seem to be different people at different times, he called this is called 'the bundle theory of the self', we are fragmented and Hume never resolved the matter of our being a coherent psychological being.

Therefore I would maintain that our psychological community is important and agree with Hume that it is not cohesive over time. I would suggest the following Marx:

> 'Consciousness does not determine being, but rather social being determines consciousness.
>
> Marx.

2) State and access the argument from design.

The argument from design is made as a rational justification for the existence of a Deity. It is stronger than the argument by faith alone, called fideism. This is because knowledge demands evidence and a theist is on stronger ground if they can employ reasoned arguments rather than a Kierkegaardian 'leap of faith' or 'Pascal' Wager'. The essential concept of argument from design is that there is an argument by analogy from the design in the world and an intelligent designer of the world who is called God.

Therefore in *Dialogues concerning Natural Religion* as the world was in tumult intellectually after the Enlightenment Hume posed the position in the form which Plato employed in his discourses, the 'Socratic discourse' when an philosophical argument is talked through but in order to how the weakness of one.

Cleanthes and Philo dispute the merits off the arguments from design. Firstly Cleanthes argue s that the world resembles one large machine, The argument follows that human beings create structures such as houses and they use intelligence and planning to do so. Therefore it follows by analogy that there must be an intelligent designer of the world who we can call God.

For an argument by analogy to be held two steps are miscarry 1) the uncontroversial case A must be true and there must be an similar 'carry over' to the controversial case B, it must also be true that there is a difference between case A and B or there could not be an analogy to answer,. Thus in an argument from design there must be order in the world which carries over to an intelligent designer who is called God. In the case of Cleanthes and Philo points out two weaknesses, a) there may be a team of builders who constructs the house and for this intelligent design to carry over to a monotheistic God, there could only be one and b) there is ample dissimilitude to make the analogy weak.

William Paley attempted to answer these weaknesses by using the Watch Makers Analogy

Premise 1. A watch is found on a beach it shows evidence of precise design.

Premise 2. The world also shows evidence of precise order. An eye.

Conclusion There is an intelligent designer of the world and we call (him) God.

But although this position has greater cogency as an analogy because of its 'functionality and precision' it was not held with the development of evolutionary science by Darwin and in particular the method of 'natural selection'. Thus biological organisms were self-selective and self- generating. This to quote Darken made the 'watch maker blind'

However does this explain who the creation of life came about in the first place Swinburne argued for a 'fine-tuning argument, i.e. that the cosmological constants needed to create the universe could have come together out of contingency, there had to be 'fine-tuning' and thus a Designer. Against this one could argue that if one bought a ticket in a lottery and won it would be by chance. And maybe the world is not a good outcome as argued Schopenhauer

3) Compare Rawls and Nozick on distributive justice in the context of social mobility.

John Rawls 'A Theory of Justice' (1971) was an attempt to answer the utilitarian position from within the Liberal tradition but with egalitarianism as an inherent aspect.

For Rawls if you were born with a talent you would deserve benefits from the excising of that talent, but his was a significant and revolutionary piece of political philosophy. It deals with the question of 'distributive justice' i.e. who should get what and in what circumstances. In order to develop his innovatory ideas he developed a particular method to answer this problem. How can one start to answer the question of who gets what? Rawls used a unique methodology:

1) The Original Position. This is a thought experiment in which a person does not know their talents, disabilities but has a basic knowledge of economics and politics.

2) The Veil of Ignorance: this is the technique whereby we capacities are hidden.

Rawls thought that if his thought experiment was conducted successfully then two basic principles would be discerned which were differentiated by the 'lexical principle'.

The first of these is the Liberty Principle i.e. everyone has the right to freedom and protection and to allow self-fulfilment or in Aristotle's a term *eudemonia*. He was also influenced by Kantian deontological

ethics in that the universiability principle was significant. This leads to his second principle which has two components:
a) Social Equality .and b) 'maximise the minimum' in which the worst off are given the best outcomes in worst situation. Therefore he ordered that we should live in a patterned society in which individual talent is rewarded but the most vulnerable protected. His was a model of meritocratic welfarism.

Answering Rawls Nozick in his *Anarchy, the State and Utopia* (1974) argued that, parodying Marx's

'From each according to need to each according to his abilities'.

Marx.

Argued:

'From each according to his chances to each according to each to what they are given.'

his book however was an answer directly to Rawls. He develops a method with a 'thought experiment'. Wilt Chamberlin, an American baseball player, is given 25c for each appearance, he is good at his career and people decide to spend their e money on seeing him. He accumulates $250.00 which is more than others in his society. For Nozick this movement away from a pattern society D1 where people have their money controlled to D2 where people freely spend money on whoever has the best talents or products. In D2 there will not be patterning indeed Nozick argues that paying taxes to 'forced labour'.

A problem with Rawls is that he presupposes certain aspects of Liberalism; individual or at least not 'social' ownership of the means of production and the individual as an agent as opposed to the social.

A problem with Nozick is he almost returns to the State of Nature described by Thomas Hobbes in *'The Leviathan'*

'a warre of every man upon all'.

Rather a solution I would argue that Rawls is an advance in that the state exists with the Difference Principle to protect the vulnerable and against Nozick who argues only for 'a night watchman state' where talents are not necessary rewarded but only the strongest and most ruthless succeed.

Nigel Pearce

Is functionalism a viable materialist theory of mind?

In order to answer whether functionalism is a viable materialist theory of the mind I shall consider a number of philosophical perspectives. Firstly, I will ask 'what is it to think' and look at how Descartes conceived the problem, then examine the Physical Monist responses, the variants of Mind- Brain Identity Theory, how this is answered by and developed by functionalism, Thomas Nagel's objection to this involving Qualia and finally an attempted solution in a Dialectical Materialist Correspondence Theory of the mind. I will find that a dialectical materialist model of thought answers both the problem of the nature of consciousness and the complex nature of its interaction in a persuasive manner.

Firstly what is thought, the answer on first examination appears straightforward:

I think, therefore I am. (Cogito Ergo Sum).
- Descartes Meditations in Cottingham (2011) p223.

But it is not so rudimentary for indeed Descartes arrived at his definition of being or consciousness through the devastation of 'self'. What we would call 'Cartesian Doubt' or 'The Method of Doubt'. Once he and is he is the 'I' of the first person, had believed the only way the 'Evil Genius' could not deceive the 'I' into believing he didn't exist was by knowing he doubted the 'thought' of his being and therefore he knew that he 'thought'. Therefore for Descartes:

Premise 1 I I can doubt that I have a body.

Premise 2, I cannot doubt I think

Conclusion. Therefore my consciousness and my body are separate.

Therefore this creates the problem of Cartesian Dualism which is both a question of consciousness and another related question of how consciousness and the body interact. Indeed it goes to the essence of the matter what is the relationship between thought and reality? Descartes had argued there were two separate substances 'mind' and 'body', although they interact. This is what modern Philosophy of the Mind has designated substance dualism and has attempted to answer and it has done so by maintaining a Material Monism, that there is one sort of 'stuff' in the universe. This first attempt was called Materialism. With the advances of science, in particular, physics, it claimed that matter as 'stuff' is both more complex including for example light waves and sub-atomic particles, this refined perspective is called 'Physicalism'. It believes for example that angels and fairies don't exist because they are not discernible as physical matter, not even as fields of energy. This in turns led to Mind-Brain Identity Theory sometimes called Reductive Materialism were a direct correlation was seen between mind and brain states, i.e.

CFS + CFS [Where CFS = C-Fibres Stimulation].
In other words when a cluster of electrons stimulates C- fibres in my mind they stimulate C- fibres in my brain and vice versa , they were one and the same thing C- fibres, This view was advanced by Smart (1959). Smart (1960) argued for materialism as follows:

By "materialism" I mean there I nothing in the world
over and above that postulated by physics…
It will now become clear why I define materialism in the way I have done above. I am concerned to deny in the world there are Non-physical entities and non-physical laws. In particular I wish to deny psychophysical dualism.'

Smart (1960) pp. 651-652.

Let me now explain the difference between a 'type and a 'token' in philosophical usage. 'Shandy is a cat. The cat is the 'type' while Shady is the 'token' or again you walk into my flat with a copy of Dostoevsky 'Crime and Punishment' but there is also my copy on my desk, they are both the 'type' of the book 'Crime and Punishment', but we have two copies or 'tokens' of the book, yours and mine. Having defined 'types' and 'token' I shall return to Mind- Brain 'Type' Identity Theory.

C fibres = C fibres in Jones the human
But in a 'possible world' or 'imagined world' there could as Hilary Putman (1967) argued be the possibility of something like M – fibres belonging to Martians. Therefore you could have:

Pain =   C- fibres = C –fibres for Jones the human.

Pain =   M- fibres + M fibres for a Martian.

This is known as 'multiple realization problem', because you can cannot 'intuitively' say in a 'possible world' that there is not another being say made of silicone. It is possible to pursue Type/Type chauvinism where the type of pain in C-fibre stimulation would be the only realized pain, in C-fibres the human', but this is counter intuitive. The problem of 'multi-reliability' is in turn addressed by Functionalism. I shall delineate this branch of the philosophy of the mind in more detail below.

However it is necessary to maintain that both Mind-Brain Identity theory and Functionalism is predicated on the premise that matter is discernible through the process of the scientific endeavour, that is, by the process of inductive logic, observation, verification and replication which, it is claimed, ascertain that 'matter' in its various manifestations is the only substance that exists. This is in contradiction to Idealism which in its pure form in the philosophy of the mind, Subjective Idealism, sees only ideas and abstractions as existing and runs the error of the 'slippery slope argument':

Premise 1 A is an X

Premise 2 There are no differences between A and B

Conclusion B is an X.

Hence the ramifications for consciousness in regard of Materialism and Subjective Idealism or Solipsism are as follows I would argue:
Premise 1 Mind is the world
Premise 2 There is no difference between the mind and my consciousness
Conclusion. My consciousness is the world.

Here we can see how a non-materialist theory of the mind leads to an almost 'psychotic' state of awareness in that the boundary between the individual's consciousnesses and 'the world' which Physicists, correctly in my view, call external material reality merges. In the form of 'Objective Idealism' the 'Absolute Idea' is often associated with the transcendent deity, a form of substance dualism where a person's ideas and the Absolute Idea of God, which is that claim maintains qualitatively different from the ideas of people are separated or bifurcated. But the deity in this sense has an underived meaning; it exists 'in and of itself'.
Returning to the central question. I illustrated how 'multiple realizations' created a problem that Physicalist Mind-Brain Identity theory in the CFS (C-Fibre Stimulation) model. This is developed by functionalism by creating a model, called a Functional Profile which treats pain, not notice what it is like to be in pain, they are not interested in what goes on inside the mind, rather   about how something, in this case pain and now it (pain) 'is 'realized'. Therefore this model of a Functional Profile is employed by functionalists:

Input	A-fibres	Output
(Trap my finger in a door)	B-fibers	(Wince/ shout).
	C-fibres	
	PAIN CENTRE.	

Hence because A fibres, B fibres and C fibres here all belong to the same Functional Profile they are all   realized' by the same physical realizer. This is because for David Lewis this 'functional' or causal role is what we know at our best current knowledge of the scientific enterprise, physics
Because the functionalist model can explain the multiple realization of different pain fibers through the method of a particular 'function' Functional Profile, it can therefore be seen correctly as an advance on the Mind-Brain Type Identity Model. Therefore in David Lewis's model:
'1. Experiences defined by causal roles.
 2. Explanatory adequacy of physics.'
        - Matravers (2011) p.63.
However following Thomas Nagel there is an unanswered question and that is 'what is it like to be conscious'
the act that an organism has conscious experience at all means,

basically, that there is something it is like to be that organism. ... fundamentally an organism has conscious mental states if and only if there is something it is like to be that organism — something it is like for the organism.

>   - T. Nagel, 'What is it like to be a bat?' repr. In *Mortal Questions* (Cambridge University Press, Cambridge, 1979), p. 166.

This, i.e. what it is like for the organism, is the subjective character or quality of experience. Indeed can I ever subjectively comprehend or 'feel "what it is like to be a bat'. In a word 'no'. At least not within the 'conversation' in which it is posited, that of scientifically knowable states of consciousness because by their very nature of the discourse it measures and collects objective information about material stuff not states of 'what it is like to' or qualia for these states are subjective. The bat knows what it is like when he cannot find fruit to eat, hunger. I can understand what hunger is, but, I argue, I cannot penetrate the consciousness of a bat and know what it feels to be hungry because we are different beings need our physiologies are different. Thus a counter argument against for a viable materialist theory of the mind once established cannot by its nature as it is objective understand stuff like 'qualia'. This position is termed 'Property Dualism', that is, the mental and a physical have different properties and should as a consequence be discerned distinct. Essentially Nagel is arguing that science and in particular physics is concerned with the objective and it is not proved that in should attempt to explain the subjective.

However I conclude that a Dialectical Materialist Correspondence Theory does provide the beginning of a solution. This is my basic contention which I shall elaborate upon and argue through. The genesis of this position of a dialectical materialist correspondence theory of the Mind and its interaction with 'the nature of the things we perceive is generated here:

Knowledge can be used... in human practice... only then it reflects truth which is independent of him. For the materialist the 'success' of practice proofs the *correspondence between our ideas and the objective nature of the things we perceive*[1]*.'*

>   - Marx & Engels (1976) p 126.

Lenin elaborates this thesis in *Materialism and Empirico-Criticism*: Matter is a philosophical category denoting the objective reality which is given by a particular set of sensations, and which is copied, photographed and reflected by our sensations, while existing independently of thought.'

>   - Lenin (1947) p.116.

---

[1] My italics.

Hence we can see a model which is neither deterministic nor simply reflective. It attempts to explain the complex nature of the relationship between consciousness and substance dualism by understanding a cognitive interaction model as follows:

Abstraction/ Cognition

Concrete reality Praxis.

Dialectical Tension

Therefore for this model of the theory of the mind, that is, the nature of consciousness and its relationship to the brain and matter as 'an active sensory activity' (Marx).

I have delineated the problem of the philosophy of the mind as understood by early modern and modern philosophy, illustrated the rise and apparent triumph of physical Monism, how allowed Mind-Brain Type Identity theory, shown how the problem of multiple realization created problems for that model, examined an example of the problem of 'slippery slope argument in relationship to the relationship between thought and matter in particular solipsism, looked to how functionalism has attempted to provide a viable materialist theory of the mind, illustrated an objection by Thomas Nagel and attempted a solution to the problem in the light of Alex Callinicos (1983) *Marxism and Philosophy* and John Molyneux (2012) *The point is to change it: an introduction to Marxist Philosophy* and the application of the question of ;correspondence theory to the development of Marxist Philosophy generally in all areas, both Callinicos and Molyneux gave contributed in the last decades.

I shall leave the last word with Lenin commenting on Hegel in his *Philosophical Notebooks:*

Life gives rise in the brain. Nature is reflected in the human brain, by checking and applying the correctness of these techniques, man arrives at objective truth.

- Lenin Collected Works, Vol 38, p201

I would maintain the dialectical materialist theory of mind and reality is a persuasive one because it illustrates complexified materialism.

Bibliography.

Callinicos, Alex (1983) *Marxism and Philosophy*, Oxford, Clarendon Press.
Cottingham, John (2011) *Western Philosophy: An Anthology*, Oxford, Blackwell.
Descartes, R (1988) *Selected Philosophical Writings* edited and translated by J Cottingham, R.Stoothal and Murdoch. Cambridge, Cambridge University Press.
Lenin. V.I. (1977) *Collected Works volume 38 'Philosophical Notebooks*, Moscow, Progress Publishers.
Lenin, V. I (1947) *Materialism and Empirico Criticism,* Moscow, Foreign Languages Press.
Marx, K & Engels, F (1976*) Collected Works,* London, Lawrence and Wishart.
Matravers, Derek (2011) *Mind Book 5 A222 Exploring Philosophy*, Milton Keynes, The Open University.
Molyneux, J (2012) *The point is to change: it: An introduction to Marxist Philosophy*, Bookmarks, And London
Nagel, Thomas 'What is it like to be a bat? 'Repr. In *Mortal Questions* (Cambridge University Press, Cambridge, 1979), p. 166.
Smart .J.C. *The Journal of Philosophy, Vol 60, No.22, American Philosophical Association* (OCT 24), 1963 pp. 652-652

Is the self a fiction, as David Hume argues?

   This thesis will contend firstly it is necessary to understand Hume's claims and the counterarguments in the context of the 'conversation' of ideas in which they took place and that the ideas of the empiricists generally represented a clear advantage over the metaphysics of the Cambridge Platonists who Locke was engaged in debate with. Also they were based on the inductive logic of the newly discover methods of the natural sciences, principally observation and experimentation, a weakness would be the reductio ad absurdum of believing in an 'eternal' world which can be ascertained by measurement and in contradiction that this world can only be 'experienced' by the 'subject'. To transcend that 'experience' by reason would seem to be a concession to rationalists who believe in deductive logic. I shall examine   Hume's claim that the self is a fiction which can be understood in terms of a reaction to John Locke's ideas regarding 'personal identity' and that Hume 'bundle theory of the self' can be comprehended only as existing within the tradition which has a Cartesian beginning. I shall argue that Hume's conceptualization of the self was an advance in philosophy and informed a significant philosophical current which remains active contemporarily and that Hume's argument that the 'self was a fiction' is proved within the parameters of empiricism but its consequences in terms of the rejection of later 'correspondence theory' where the logical outcome of Hume's analysis taken to its conclusion. I shall then conclude.

   'The outcome of Hume's Enquiry was exceedingly ironic.
   He began with the intention of finding out what sensory
   evidence there was for our fundamental belief about the
   world. He ended up detaching those beliefs from their
   foundation in objective reality.'

                                   -    Novack (1971) p 80.

   I argue from the position that the material and the ideological circumstances which produced 'Early Modern British Empiricism' created a dominant and progressive if an equivocal philosophy attached to the Scientific Revolution and its confederates and was an advance. It was in contrast to those like the Platonists who looked to 'truth from authority' for guidance. In opposition to Innatism a key aspect of both Locke and Hume thought was an, apparent, reliance on inductive reasoning in natural science both as the origin of knowledge and methodology of achieving it. Therefore for Hume the human mind would become the area for what Grayling (ed. 2007 p542) calls 'philosophical psychology'. However Hume would utilise both sense-experience and introspection in his quest for an epistemology of the self. Thus although Locke rejected Innatism with his tabula rasa he was not able to move beyond the atomized individual as the starting point which was the 'conversation' which David Hume was working within and this is consistent with their epoch. As A. C. Grayling argues:

(Locke) accepted from Descartes, and transmitted to the empiricist tradition, the assumption that the right place to start an inquiry into the nature and extent of knowledge is the private contents of the individual consciousness. The empiricist twist is to place reliance on the data of sense.'

-                    Grayling (2007) p 507.

John Hume's formulation of 'the self' as fiction' can be seen as answering the question left unanswered by Locke if personal identity is 'consciousness of self alone' with a maintenance of memory and action which is in turn 'forensic' which he illustrates using the Prince and the Cobbler 'thought-experiment:

'For should the Soul of a Prince, carrying with it the consciousness of the prince's past life, enter and inform the body of a cobbler as soon as deserted by his own soul, everyone sees, he would the same person with the prince, accountable only for the prince's actions: But who would say it was the same man? The body too goes to the making of the man and would, I guess, to every body determine the man in this case, wherein the soul, with all its princely thoughts about it, would not make another man: But he would be the same cobbler to every one besides himself. I know that in the ordinary way of speaking, the same person, and the same man, stand for one and the same thing.'

- Locke in Cottingham (2008) p 278.

This can be expressed as person B (on Wednesday is identical with person A (on Tuesday) if B can remember being A.

This can be rearticulated in a similar thought experiment which also relies on the Ship of Thebes that is derived from the writings of Petrarch in that it also asks a question of continence over time and identity. So if the man down the street has my awareness and memories, but his body then he is me as a 'person'. However if I had committed a crime he may be found culpable in a legal court as he is in his body that Locke called a 'man'? Nevertheless I would be morally responsible ultimately. However what would the case if I had dreamt it all and woke the next day?' I think according to Locke I would be a different 'person. This can be expressed as A=B B=C A does not equal C. But Reid uses a thought-experiment (Reid, 2002 (1785), p 276) which contradicts Locke and illustrates that he out this lacks a transitive relation and is therefore reductio ad absurdum. Reid argues that logically A=B, B=C and therefore A=C, a syllogism.

Now I will look at Hume's epistemology in some detail and then relate it to his theory of the self as a 'fiction'. Locke had established a theory of identity which was one of consciousness sustained by the continuance of memory. Hume asks a more rudimentary question about the nature of the self in relation to the external world and how we experience it i.e. our awareness of the world as 'object' and how the 'subject' interacts with the world. Firstly he argues that all our sense experiences are 'perceptions'. These literally make an 'impression' on the mind. The impression then is represented in the mind as an idea. Therefore he uses the thought experiment of a blind man who has never seen a colour and because he has not had the 'impression' of that colour' he cannot have an 'idea' or copy of it. So if I had never seen a black and white chess board I would not have the information necessary to know without pain of contradiction what one looked like, I could guess but that would not be an adequate proof and self-evidently I would make errors if I tried to play a game of chess. Now to adapt another of Hume's thought experiments: I have seen a chequered 64 square board and I have seem a set of chess pieces; I can 'imagine' how they would look, but I wouldn't be able to play. Hume uses the example of the gold mountain to a similar purpose.

Hume makes a contrast between 'simple; and 'complex' ideas, so to have the idea of gold and the idea of a mountain are 'simple ideas', but to 'imagine' the idea of a gold mountain is a complex idea which is a combination of 'simple' ideas. However how does this help us locate the self? For Hume we 'introspect' and what is there? 'nothing but a bundle or collections of different perceptions'

Hume {1739-40} in Cottingham (2008) p 286.

in flux. Therefore for Hume we are wrong if we think we have a continuing identify over time. Rather our sense of self is like a theatre with actors going across the stage. The actors are our impressions caused by our perceptions but there is not a stage. We are just a bundle of experiences created by our perceptions of the world. Therefore the self is a fiction as Hume argues:

'it is plain, that in the course of our thinking, and in the constant
revolution of our ideas, our imagination runs easily from one
idea to any other that resembles it, and that this quality alone
is to the fancy a sufficient bond and association. It is likewise
evident those as the senses, in changing their objects, are
necessitated to change them regularly, and take them as
they lie contiguous to each other, the imagination must by long
custom acquire the same method of thinking, and run along the
parts of space and time in conceiving its objects."

-              ibid p.287

These points invite two questions: 1) what is the casual relation i.e. how do I know the mountain will be gold when I look at it and 2) what has caused me to believe erroneously that I had a 'self' which had the 'consciousness of an 'idea' that remained unchanging, Why did I believe in the 'fiction' of my 'self'?

The former is answered by Hume in this way. A statement must rely on either a priori knowledge such as mathematics 1+1 = 2 or a posteriori knowledge i.e. that which is 'after experience'. This is called Hume's Fork and he argues if neither of these proofs is offered, either 'abstract reasoning' or 'matter of fact' then:

'No. Commit it to the flames. It is nothing but sophistry and illusion.'

Hume (2008) {1748] p120.

In regard of the second point the 'self as a fiction' or a bundle of different ideas is answered by Hume in this way. Why are there 'bundles', what holds them together? Nothing because when I introspect there is just nothing and when I look at the world just a stream of fleeting impressions. Hume claims that there could be some causal principle in the world, the belief that A causes B and therefore B must cause A. But it could not be a proof as for Hume we merely expect it to happen as we expect the sun to rise.

I would argue that Hume began with the ambiguity present in all empiricism that they postulate the eternal world but cannot proof objectively its existence it can only be proved by impressions and there are problems here a) who generates the experience and b) what are the objects or things which are senses tell us about. Hume questions the notion of the 'subject' itself, the self itself is a fiction and not to be supported by the experience of the of Berkeley's spiritual 'substance'. What are we left with, Novak's argues that:

'Hume's scepticism corroded the internal ties of their (the empiricists) synthesis of ideas, Thereafter empiricism doubted everything on principle.'

Novack (1971) p 82.

Blackburn (2008) argues Hume on self as fiction prefigures Nietzsche who he quotes:

'What separates me most deeply from metaphysicians is: I don't concede that the 'I' thinks. Instead, I take I itself to be a construction for thinking...in other words only a regulative fiction with the help of some kind of constancy and thus 'knowability' is inserted into, invented into, a world of becoming.'

Nietzsche (2003) pp. 20-1.

One remedy to the problems of empiricism in general and particularly Hume's position on the 'self as fiction' relies on 'correspondence of truth theory' by creating a dialectical relationship between 'subject' and 'object':

'Life gives rise to the brain. Nature is reflected in the human brain. By checking and applying the correctness of these reflections in his practice and his truth, man arrives at objective truth.'

V.I. Lenin (1977) Collected Works, p 201.

Thus I am arguing for a complexified version of Parfit's Reductionism which he delineates as:

"On the Reductionist View, each person's existence just involves the existence of a brain and body, the doing of certain

26

deeds, the thinking of certain thoughts, the occurrence of certain experiences, and so on.'

Derek Parfit (1986), Reasons and Persons, p. 211.

Hence I would argue that the 'Self' as an 'individual' entity is indeed a fiction within the boundaries of the man of empiricism, but is not when man is interacting with Nature and in an assemblage of social relations and when he is made concrete by his association with 'Nature' and 'the gaze' of others.

Bibliography.

Blackburn, S (2008) How to Read Hume, London, Granta.

Cottingham, J ed (2008) Western Philosophy: An Anthology, Oxford, Blackwell Publishing.

Grayling, A.C. ed (2007) Philosophy 1: a guide through the subject, Oxford University Press.

Hume, D (2008) {1748} An Enquiry Concerning Human Understanding, Oxford,

Oxford University Press, world Classics.

Lenin, V, I (1977) Collected Works, Vol 38, Moscow, Progress Publishers.

Nietzsche, F, (2003) Writings from the Late Notebooks, ed Rudiger Bittner, trans.

Kate Sturge (Cambridge, Cambridge University Press.

Novack (1971) Empiricism and its Evolution: a Marxist view, New York, Pathfinder.

Parfit, D (1986) Reasons and Persons Oxford: Oxford University Press

Reid, T (2002) {1785} Essays on the Individual Powers of Man (ed).

D. R. Brookes, University Park, Pennsylvania, Pennsylvania State University Press.

Warburton, N (2011) The Self Book 1 Open University A222 Exploring Philosophy,

Milton Keynes, The Open University.

Are analogies between the state/citizen relation and the parent/child relation robust enough to explain a citizen's obligation to the state?

An analogy of the state/citizen relation to the parent/child relation is articulated by Plato in a Socratic dialogue in Crito:

What complaint, pray, do you have against the city and ourselves? that you should now attempt to destroy us? Was it not we who gave you birth

Plato (1997) p. 73.

The question of whether an analogy between the state/citizen and parent/child explain the citizen's obligations to the state is central to this question. Therefore I will examine the structure of arguments by analogy. I will do this by examining another significant argument by analogy that of William Paley for argument from design. The argument by analogy requires three components. That the first or 'uncontroversial case' must be held, second that there is not a dis-analogy between the 'uncontroversial case and the 'controversial case' and third for an argument by analogy there is inherently the necessity for the first or 'uncontroversial case' and the second or 'controversial case' to be differentiated or there would be no possible analogy. Therefore it follows that if in the example of Paley's thought experiment if you were walking on a beach and you find a watch and he makes an analogy between the working of the watch and because they interact in an intelligent or 'functional way' he can attempt to make the case for argue from design between the watch/world and designer/God. There must be evidence of the functionality of the watch for some form of design to be held to exist, if there was no evidence of function in the watch there can be no analogy with the world, the analogy would fall on the first case. So we can argue the functionality of the watch generates the necessity of a designer. Then the argument follows that we notice evidence of design in the world, there seems to be evidence of complex design in the human eye or in the composition of a leaf of grass. Paley then extrapolates from this first case to an analogous leap to the necessity for there to be a Designer of the human eye of the world of nature, the analogy seems to work. The 'uncontroversial case' is held, there is an analogy between their being a designer of the watch and functionality, we perceive design or function in the world. Therefore there must be a designer who made the watch and thus a Designer who created ordered systems in the world of Nature, an Intelligent Designer who the argument goes is God. Now this works as an argument by analogy because the first case stands and the inference to its conclusion is not dis-analogous and the watch and the world are not the same thing so there is an analogy to be answered. But it is an argument from induction in that we generalize from the evidence to a conclusion. An argument from analogy is not a deductively valid argument. As an example of how an analogy functions William Paley's is a good one, it collapsed though when Darwin proved that species are generated by 'natural selection. I have illustrated my argument in this way in order to show, by way of an example how an argument by analogy is structured.

As I have looked at the mechanics of an argument by analogy is some detail I shall now apply that specifically to the question of the robustness or not of the child/parent analogy is to the citizen/state in Plato's Crito. The figure below illustrates the position:

Parent – child relation		State – citizen relation
generates	maps across to	generates
obligations of gratitude to parents from children		obligations of gratitude to the state from its citizens (political obligations)

Figure 1.2   The parent–state analogy

Pike (2011) p. 20.

The question is one of a benefits argument: a) what benefits does the hypothetical parent provide their child and if they can be carried over to b) the benefits which the state provides for its citizens. Essentially the hypothetical parent will provide a number of things, subsistence, safety and protection; These are the means of subsistence necessary for human existence as Fredrick Engels said at the funeral of Karl Marx:

Just as Darwin discovered the law of development or organic nature, so Marx discovered the law of development of human history: the simple fact, hitherto concealed by an overgrowth of ideology, that mankind must first of all eat, drink, have shelter and clothing, before it can pursue politics, science, art, religion, etc.; that therefore the production of the immediate material means, and consequently the degree of economic development attained by a given people or during a given epoch, form the foundation upon which the state institutions, the legal conceptions, art, and even the ideas on religion, of the people concerned have been evolved, and in the light of which they must, therefore, be explained, instead of vice versa, as had hitherto been the case.

Engels, [1883] (1973) p 426

Therefore the benefits the parents give the child are analogous if they are reproduced by the state to the citizen. If this works thinkers like John Rawls believe that the State should 'maximise the minimum' to create the condition in which the citizen may have the opportunity to experience Aristotelian flourishing or eudemonia. Aristotle argued that we are 'political animals' that is we live in the polis which can be defined broadly as a state with a sense of community. He argued further that: the state came into being as a means to protect life, it continues in existence in order to secure the good life.

Aristotle, in Cottingham (2011) p 622.

In a manner this begs the question as it should (a) parent/state must provide benefits in order for (b) the child/ citizen to prosper for the analogy to pass the first case. If it does not do this there are no benefits then there is no case to answer. It is certainly true in the present economic circumstances the (a) may be struggling rather with the consequence of that which leads to (b) hardship, welfare cuts. Therefore for a benefits argument to work by analogy the benefits must be apparent in the first case and carried over in the second. That is my basic structure. I would argue that it can fail in the first case, because you cannot argue that a hypothetical parent-child relation is consistent enough once you remove the bonds of patriarchal authority. Therefore if this fails Socrates has no obligations to Athens, he may feel he has duties of a Kantian nature but these are not obligations if the analogy has failed. Once patriarchal authority is answered there is no 'benefits argument' between parent and child. It would be the same if Paley's watch wasn't functional; it doesn't 'work' as philosophical analogy. Secondly, the first and second case is dis-analogous because tone is an objective relationship and the other, subjective.

I shall examine a number of philosophical perspectives and a methodology to sketch a context of the citizen's obligation is central to the questions to the state in relation to the question of the structure of 'argument by analogy'. John Rawls (1971) A Theory of Justice attempted to create the theoretical framework for a 'fair-play' argument with his 'Difference Principle':

Alex Callinicos points out that in Rawls (1971) A Theory of Justice:

The difference principle which involves a deeper form of equality than equality of opportunity, at least as normally understood. Like many revolutionary works, A Theory of Justice is deeply embedded in the tradition from which it emerged- in this case classical liberalism.

, and also that in order to understand:

A theory is often best understood by considering what it is written against. In Rawls case this is Unitarianism.

Callinicos (2007) p.42.

This tendency was best represented by its founder, Jeremy Bentham

An action then may be said to be comfortable to the principle ...when the tendency it has to augment the happiness of the community is greater than to diminish it.

Bentham (1982) pp12-13

Philosophical anarchists argue that no political obligations can be successfully held between the citizen and the state. Marxist political philosophers would present a different perspective and a different methodology. A Liberal like John Locke would presume there are obligations on both sides both the citizen and the state. Locke makes the point that a citizen may give 'tacit consent' to the authority of the state:

>...whether it be barely travelling feely on the highway...
>
> Locke, 1690, in Cottingham (2011) p. 640.

Rawls claims to have addressed these questions while Libertarians on the political New Right like David Novack in turn argued against his principle of 'maximize the minimum', the best outcomes in the worst case, by arguing for a state to exist merely as a guardian of property rights.

An analogy of the state/citizen relation to the parent/child relation is articulated in Plato Crito and began a discourse on the nature of the relationship between citizen and the state which is at the core of Western political philosophy. In this way it is something akin to the organic analogies in the human. The two relationships which Plato characterises in Crito, by analogies, are firstly that of the relationship of children to their parents and secondly the relationship of the slave to the master. I shall concentrate on the former but recognize the latter in this dialectic.

Plato uses the case of the aging Socrates condemned to death by the state for denying the state religion and spreading dissident concepts amongst the youth to explore the nature of this argument from analogy. However is there a benefits argument to be had in the parent/child and citizen/state relationship? What rights and obligations are involved? So is any relationship of an implicit nature as Locke argues is not convincing for not many make a conscious and explicit commitment to the state. Do the citizenry rather give up their sovereignty to an Absolute Ruler in return for protection from a life which would otherwise be 'a warre of all on all' which would be 'nasty and brutish and short' Hobbes argued in his important text ,'The Leviathan'. I would argue however it is a process of socio-historical Necessity that defines the citizen's orientation to the state:

> It is not the consciousness of men that determines their being, but, on the contrary, their social being determines their consciousness.

> Marx [1857] (2007) p. 425

My findings are: 1) if patriarchal authority is not accepted then in the first case this analogy fails, 2) the analogy is not robust in-itself i.e. it does not 'carry-over' and 3) if positions #1 and #2 are held even if you accept patriarchal authority then you should bit the bullet and argue for a necessary 'social transformation'. This is required because even if the analogy works as benefits/fair-play argument which is really neo-Liberalism and Rosa Luxemburg has argued eloquently liberalism or the fair-play/benefits argument can be articulated as:

the hard core of social inequality and lack of freedom hidden under the sweet shell of formal equality and freedom.'

Luxemburg (1970) p.393.

Hence we are left with a dilemma. I have argued that the analogy in question is not robust, Rawls only adapts liberalism and Novack rejects any obligation on the state except 'night-watchman'. A solution to the problem of the failure of the child/parent analogy with citizen/ state would be a workers state acting and controlled by the majority which then 'withers away' (Engels) leaving Communism as the true dawn of human History where there would be a genuine benefits to all, socialized benefits in a socialized state:

'From each according to his abilities too each according to their needs'

Marx [1875] (2007) p.615.

Bibliography.

Aristotle (300 BC) Politics in Cottingham, Western Philosophy: an anthology, Oxford, Blackwell Publishing.

Bentham, J (1982) An Introduction to the Principles of morals and Legislation, London.

Callinicos, A (2007) Equality, Cambridge, Polity Press.

Cottingham, J (2011) [ed] Western Philosophy: an anthology, Oxford, Blackwell.

Engels, F [1883] (1973) Marx & Engels Selected Works, London, Lawrence and Wishart.

Locke, J (1690) Second Treatise of Civil Government in Cottingham (2011) [ed] Western Philosophy: an anthology, Oxford, Blackwell Publishers.

Luxemburg, R (1970) Rosa Luxemburg Speaks, New York.

Marx, K [1875] (2007) Critique of the Gotha Programme in Karl Marx Selected Writings, Oxford, Oxford University Press

Marx, K [1875] (2007) Preface to the Critique of Political Economy in Karl Marx Selected Writings, Oxford. Oxford University Press

Pike, J (2011) Exploring Philosophy, Book 6 Political Philosophy, Milton Keynes, The Open University,

Plato (1995) Defence of Socrates, Euthyphro and Crito. Oxford, Oxford World Classics.

What is Judith Jarvis Thomson's 'famous violinist' analogy supposed to show? Does it?

This thesis will describe and evaluate the 'famous violinist' analogy which was a thought-experiment presented by Judith Jarvis Thomson (1971). In order to do this it is necessary to delineate the argument made by Thomson, illustrate the 'famous violinist' analogy in the context of her argument and also consider whether the analogy is valid within the context of the persuasiveness of analogous logic. Having described the argument I shall access if it can be allowed by deductive logic. However Thomson's thesis is one using applied ethics which can only be comprehended for the purposes of evaluation within the 'conversation' of Western moral philosophy. It is specific to the debate regarding abortion but as an argument must be tested for validity and soundness as a piece of logic. Thomson's paper was not centred on the question of the nature of the foetus in particular as were the cases with other pro-choice feminists like Warren (1973). Both Warren and Thomson were replying to a social discourse in regard of abortion, they were therefore applying ethical philosophy to a pertinent social question. The general question was in regard to the moral permissibility of abortion with the anti-abortionists arguing they were no grounds on which it was 'morally' allowed. The argument which Thomson attempts to answer is a syllogism employed by anti-abortionists:

Premise 1 Killing people is wrong.

Premise 2 A foetuses is a person.

Conclusion. Therefore killing a foetus is wrong and hence abortion is not morally permissible.

This fundamental syllogism is valid because its premises are correctly inferred to the conclusion and therefore it is sound. However it relies on a priori 'truths' 1) That it is wrong to kill and 2) That a foetus is a person. It is answered by many feminists who question 'Essentialism'. Simone de Beauvoir The Second Sex (1953) was a seminal philosopher here:

'One is not born, but rather one becomes a woman'

de Beauvoir (1953) bk 2, p 4, ch 1.

Hence once 'Essentialism' was rejected an area of freedom opens. Premise 2 is attacked by Warren because, she argued, the foetus is not a 'person' as it is not a member of the 'moral community' (Warren (1973), p 43). So for Warren the following syllogism was advanced:

Premise 1 It is wrong to kill something if it is a person.

Premise 2 Foetuses are not people.

Conclusion It is not wrong to kill foetuses.

An innovation in Thomson is that she permits Premise 1 of the anti-abortionist argument, in this she resembles an 'act utilitarian', as the act of killing the foetus causes a greater decrease in pain to the woman and increases the good of both the individual woman and society. Thomson places the question of the 'rights' of the woman at the core of her position. She constructs her argument by a series of syllogisms and thought experiments of which the 'famous violinist' analogy is the most significant. How does Thomson achieve this? She begins the argument by conceding Premise 1 of the anti-abortion syllogism that was outlined earlier:

'What happens if, for the sake of argument, we allow the premise... I propose, then, we grant that the foetus is a person from the moment of conception. How does the argument go from here? Something like this, I take it. Every person has the right to life. So the foetus has the right to life...it sounds plausible. But now let me try to ask you to imagine this.'

Thomson [1971] in Cottingham (ed) (2011) p. 591.

It is here that Thomson employs her 'famous violin' analogy. However before I present this I want to comment on some questions in regard analogical thought experiments. Arguments from analogy are a specific area of philosophy. Although they are inductive they are often components of a deductive argument. A useful definition is:

'Arguing from analogy is arguing that since some things are alike In one case, they will probably be alike in another. It's most famous use was in the Design Argument...But: Wittgenstein 'How can I generalize the case so irresponsibly?''

Blackburn (ed) (2008) p.13.

I shall now describe Thomson's 'famous violinist' analogy in which she employs as an element of her argument again the anti-abortionists. She asks us to imagine (thought experiment) that we are kidnapped by a Society of Music Lovers who are aware we have the same rare blood-type as a 'famous violinist' who has kidney disease I ('she' Thomson is gender-specific) wake up in a hospital bed connected to the 'famous violinist' and this connection to him is made to allow him to sustain his life:

'Is it morally incumbent on you to accede to this situation? No doubt it would be very nice of you if you did, a great kindness. But you have to decide. But do you have to accede? What if it were not nine months, but nine years? Or longer still?'

Thomson [1971] in Cottingham (ed) (2011) p 989-990.

As a piece of analogical thinking it must prove that it has a link which is valid in the sense of 'truth bearing' or inference between the x famous violinist and the woman and y the foetus and a pregnant woman. A possible way of doing this is to ascertain 'sufficient' and 'necessary' conditions. Two tests can be used for this a) is there a 'sufficient condition': if between the two i.e. if x is met it is enough for y to stand and b) is there a 'necessary condition' for the analogy to stand is x required for y to stand. This is at the heart of the problem.

a) If there is a 'sufficient condition' then it is only required for there to be a 'loose analogy'

"Certain moral principles being, as we've said, thus seen to be true by intuition, under due conditions of reflection and thought, are unfolded into their application by further reflection and thought"
Whewel (1864), 12–13).
'loose analogy is different to an exact...explanation." (ibid).
b) If there was a 'necessary condition' for the analogy to stand it would have to show a causal relation in the way William Parley (1803) tried to conceive a direct analogy between the workings a watch, nature and a Deity.

There are excellent thought experiments like Thomson's own 'The Trolley Problem' (1986) in which she develops Philippi Foot (1967) argument if you intuitively switch a railway point to save five lives to save one would you push a large man off a bridge to prevent the trolley train killing five. Almost anyone would switch the points but to kill to save five lives I think some indeed many people would find it difficult to push the fat man off a bridge to stop the train hitting a group of people. But then 'Double Effect' is what Thomson is arguing for in her 'A Defence of Abortion' (1971). Many would do it in the heat of the moment; it would meet a sufficient condition of 'intuition' developed above. But it is not enough to make her 'famous violinist' work as a 'necessary condition'. My second criteria. For that more that intuitively weighing-up the plusses and minuses but to sit down and think through the consequences of the analogy working. If nature is like one huge machine then you can attempt to make an analogous leap to an existence of a Deity. But following Hume (1779) it fails. It is too large a leap to make after consideration. In one sits down and contemplates an act then carry it out like the woman in the 'famous violinist' analogy the methodology involved is different from making a split second decision to save five lives instead of one, I would argue. There is a consequentialist argument that can be made. I shall illustrate with a thought experiment of my own devising.

A gay man enraged by the death of a man in a homophobic attack grasp an iron bar and smashes the offices of a local far-right organization. He has behaved impulsively but with the intention of frightening the fascists to protect his friends who may out be greater both in number and in personal quality in the neighbourhood. He may have acted correctly yet without thought for the consequences which may adverse or his friends i.e. they may cause further homophobic attacks. A friend of his considers deeply the consequences of what has happened, he fears for his life and decides that attacking only the most famous fascist can he protect himself? He meets up with some radical Marxists. They then think through the situation and use their ideology as guidance for how they behave. They belief the fascists should be taught a lesson and that this will generalize   their ideology to the masses and therefore create the greater good of social change.

So the first gay man behaved like the person in both Foot (1967) and Thompson (1986) in that he acted quickly and intuitively with a degree of thought for the greater good of his community, but not with a thought through plan, I would say he could have acted out of a sufficient condition . But the second gay man has thought like the agent in Thomson (1971) he has considered his position and it is a necessary condition of him acting in this way i.e. it depends on it in the same way the agent in Thomson decided it was essential to save their own life to disconnect their kidneys from the famous violinist, so he as a necessary condition of his 'self-defence' considers 'disconnecting' the 'most famous fascist' from his means life. Have both of them contradicted themselves in that to save life it is has been taken. But this contraction is only fully shown to not to hold because from a deontological Kantian perspective. I or the agent cannot protect themselves by universalizing the principle that is acceptable to kill accept if they were suicidal in the sense of self murder. They have defeated the Categorical Imperative by adopting a false maxim, 'self-interest'

'I ought never to act except in such a way that I can also will that my maxim should become a universal law.'

Kant (1785) in Cottingham (2011) p 510.

Thomson actually goes beyond that saying it 'would be 'nice'' to act with 'ought' which is confusing in Kantian terms acting with duty, they have acted from duty, Kant favouring he latter.

So how do the group of Marxists in my thought experiment behave they are certainly not motivated by hedonism + consequence = 'act' utilitarianism, Which J.S. Mill in calls in Utilitarianism (1861):

'A doctrine worthy only of the swine'

J.S. Mill (1861) in Cottingham (2011) p 513.

However they are not motivated by Mills elitist higher pleasures v lower pleasures but rather in the words of Ferdinand Lassalle in his play Franz von Sickingen:

'Do not only show the goal, show the path as well. For so closely interwoven with one another are path and goal. That a change in one means a change in the other, And a different path gives rises to a different goal'

Lassalle in Trotsky (2011).

I would hold that there should therefore not be an analogy between the ends of woman controlling their bodies and the rights of anything outside of Warren's 'moral community', but rather dialectical interdependent and that Judith Jarvis Thomson has broken 'the law of contradiction as in Formal Logic 'A cannot be non A' i.e. you cannot be a person and not a person' which is expressed in A Defence of Abortion after the 'famous violinist' analogy. Her argument fails because of its structure:

Premise 1 The violinist is a person

Premise 2 You may disconnect yourself from the violinist

Conclusion Therefore it is permissible to kill persons and hence abortion is allowed.

This argument is camera obscura of the 'extreme view' (Thomson (1971) or anti-abortionist perspective. This is a consequence of allowing the 'famous violinist' analogy.   It fails both Aristotle eudemonia and Kant's 'Golden Rule'.

Can religious experience be used to justify belief in God?

This thesis will attempt to answer the question of whether religious belief can be used to justify belief in God by employing the method of deductive logic. I shall place this 'argument' in the context of two competing view of religious experience, firstly William James who perceived it as generally positive but then deploy Jean-Paul Sartre's counter-argument of 'bad faith' . I shall use a 'thought-experiment' of my own devising to illustrate my positions. The 'argument' itself is similar to that of David Hume (1990 [1779]) and in the tradition of British Empiricism questions any form of a priori 'truth from authority' and therefore I utilise a methodology which originates in Hume who I employ and quote but also attempt to make it contemporary using examples from Kierkegaard, Swinburne, Engels and Marx. After my 'argument' has concluded that religious experiences do occur but are contrary to the laws of the natural world and are rather the projected essence of an alienated humanity I conclude with the protagonist of the 'thought-experiment' achieving an Aristotelian sense of eudemonia. Therefore firstly I would like to examine two 20th century responses to religious experience, its relationship to self and others and the consequences of the respective positions in regard of these experiences of God. I shall suggest that here the ramifications of the perspectives has a very contemporary resonance i.e. how do people behave 'authentically' in response to a religious experience of a Deity or 'Higher Power'. The contrast will be illustrated by a 'thought-experiment'. The term 'religious experience' is used quite loosely in William James (1902) The Varieties of Religious Experience. He defined this experience as a 'proof' but not in the way contemporary Catholic theologian Alasdair Macintyre does when he argued: 'Truth is tradition- constituted' (Chappell, 2011 p.151) for a particular religion. Rather for James the 'sign' of genuine religious experience was a generalized 'moral proof' rather than embracing a particular tradition. At broadly transformative experience which leads to a state of consciousness in which:

> '...one aim grows so stable as to expel definitively its previous rivals from the individual life.'

James (1902), Lecture IX p, 191.

A 'thought-experiment' could be an alcoholic going on the programme prescribed by Alcoholics Anonymous and embracing a 'Higher Power' as a solution to their addiction and thereby facilitating a personal and moral transformation. They may be deceived and deceiving as a result of this experience of the Divine. The 'onus of proof' is with those advocating the 'salvation' of my subject to the detriment of their human authenticity. Jean-Paul Sartre uses a term, 'bad faith'. Sartre defines 'bad faith' as a hiding of truth from self, an inauthenticity in the face of existential reality which is absurd because there is no Deity, following Nietzsche and 'the death of God' (Nietzsche (1882 [1977]) The Gay Science, Section 125). Paradoxically for Sartre to belief in 'bad faith' one must belief it to be true, it becomes dialectical, the victim is both the perpetrator of the deception yet also its victim because it denies him or her existential 'freedom' So at the same time the liar, as liar, believes the lie to be false, and as victim believes it to be true. So there is a contradiction in that when a person acts in 'bad faith' or self-deception believes something to be true and false at the same time. In Being and Nothingness (1976) he writes:

'Thus in order for bad faith to be possible, sincerity itself must be bad faith'

Sartre (1976) p 67

To illustrate this Sartre uses a 'thought- experiment' of a waiter who is too eager to please:

'(as he carries the food) his movement is quick and forward, a little too precise, a little too rapid.'

Sartre (1993), pp. 167-169.

To return to my 'thought-experiment', the alcoholic may believe in God or a 'Higher Power' but their zealousness may, if Sartre is correct and I think he is, reveal that they have deceived themselves, and because of the interdependent unity of opposites in dialectical formulations, others as well. I would suggest that the first position in my 'thought-experiment' is based on an enthymeme, the unstated assumption or premise being that the religious experience is necessary beneficial and that for the alcoholic to deceive themself and others is therefore simply a non sequitur, it 'does not follow'. Having explored the nature of the religious perspective from these two contrasting perspectives I shall embark on the argument by using deductive logic as understood here:

'Logic may be defined as the theory of the conditions of valid inference, or more shortly, as the theory of proof. Inference is a process by which we pass from a belief in one or more statements (the premises) to a belief in a further statement (the conclusion) whose truth, if the inference is a good one, is either guaranteed or at least made probable by the truth of the premises.'

Ree and Ormson (ed), (2005) p.211.

Hence the basic structure of my argument will be as follows:

Premise 1: A religious experience is transcendent and caused by a Divine Being, it is subjective. But it is not a hallucination.

Premise 2: The material world exists and is governed by objective laws.

Subconclusion 1: So if people have subjective experiences of God these necessary transcend or 'violate' the material world and its laws.

Premise 3: All that exists is this material world is governed by its own laws and is not transformed by the intervention of a Divine Being.

Subconclusion 2: So religious experiences are created by a transcendental God intervening in the world and are not caused by the laws of the material world.

Premise 4: As all that exists is the material world and is caused by that physical world therefore religious experiences are illusions.

Conclusion: Therefore because religious experiences are based on illusions they can be used to justify a belief in God who cannot intervene in the material world because the Deity itself is an illusion or a projection and thus it follows that objectively God does not exist.

It is necessary to contrast Natural Theology which maintains that knowledge of the Divine can be achieved through Reason and observation of the world, as in the teleological argument, in order to ascertain the existence of the Deity and another branch of the philosophy of religion which is founded in Revelation and seeks knowledge of Divinity in miracles and sacred scripture. A reliance on the later leads to fideism or a belief in 'justification by faith alone' and possibly found its highest manifestation in the philosophy of Kierkegaard who argued that people must simply make 'a leap of faith' this I would argue is another example of Sartre's 'bad faith'. However Natural Theology and Revelation are not mutually exclusive and it in the area of miracles and religious experience they overlap and interact. The key issue is Evidentialism in that it is necessary to define what evidence is appropriate to make a claim for a proof of a miracle and more pertinently to this thesis 'religious experience'. The counter-argument to Evidentialism is made by Revelation 'No one has ever seen God' (John 1:18) [1962]. However following Hume I argue in a similar vein to him:

'The plain consequence is (and it is a general maxim worthy of our attention) 'That no testimony is sufficient to establish a miracle, unless the testimony be of such kind that its falsehood would be more miraculous than the fact which it attempts to follow.'

Hume (1748) in Cottingham p 373.

Firstly as Swinburne argues:

If it seems to me that I have a glimpse of Heaven, or a vision of God that is grounds for me and others to suppose I have.'

Swinburne (1968) pp. 320-328.

So here we have an experience of a supernatural being or entity being experienced by a Fellow of the British Academy and therefore we may presume it is not a hallucination and he is sane.

Secondly we have an account of a material world that is governed by objective laws. Engels presents the argument:

'the great basic question of all philosophy…is that of thinking to being…Thus the question of the relation of thinking to being, the relation of the spirit to nature is the paramount religious question.'

Engels (1975) pp13-14.

Maurice Cornforth reinforces two points

'1. Materialism teaches that the world is by its very nature material that everything which exists comes into being on the basis of material causes, rises and develops in accordance with the laws of matter.

2. Materialism teaches that matter is objective reality existing outside and independent of the mind; and that far from the mental existing in separation from the material, everything mental or spiritual is the product of material processes.

Cornforth (1977) p 25.

Therefore I have established the first premise 1) That religious experience exists in a definable sense and the second, a position for a material analysis of reality.

Hence the Subconclusion inferred from these is that if religious experience exists it must violate the laws of the material world in the same way Hume says a miracle:

'may be accurately defined, a transgression of the law of nature by a particular violation of the Deity, or by the interposition of some invisible agent.'

Hume (2000) p.87.

It must be experienced subjectively but not be a product of insanity it must also be accompanied by a 'sense' of the Divine which is verifiable by other member of the person's culture.

Premise 3 is defined by Cornforth (1977) p.27

Materialism teaches that the world and its laws are knowable, and that while much in the material world may not be known there is no sphere of reality which lies outside of the material world. Marxist philosophy is characterised by it's absolutely consistently materialism.'

Thus I arrive at a second Subconclusion here inferred from above that if religious experience exists and cannot be the product of the material world then it must be derived from a transcendental being revealed by revelation.

My fourth premise is articulated by Marx:

'Religion is the sigh of the oppressed creature…It is the opium of the people. The abolition of religion as the illusory happiness of the people is the demand for their real happiness. To call on them to give up their illusions about their condition is to call on them to give up a condition that requires illusions.'

Marx. (1975). p2

My argument is essentially that religious experiences are illusory and a product of alienation.

This lead to my conclusion that if religious experiences occur which they do and the world is governed by material laws which it is, then these experiences must be illusions and by extrapolation God is a delusion, a product of an alienated humanity 'projecting' its essence or what the young Marx called its 'species-being; into the heavens.

In the 'thought experiment' my alcoholic subject may have had a religious experience through a 'Higher Power' and conquered his addiction, but after meeting a existentialist philosophy student who introduced him to Sartre starts drinking again but lives 'authentically'. He then goes through a 'dry' spell and has a 'genuine' spiritual experience and decides to work in a shelter for the homeless. Here he meets an old man who introduces him to Marxist philosophy. He then realizes that he was alienated from his 'true' humanity, joins a revolutionary group in order to attempt to transform the social conditions that give rise to illusions such as religion. He finally as an old man is content after reading Aristotle on eudemonia.

The argument is although people have religious experiences, they paradoxically disproof a Divinity by their illusionary nature. That a fideism based on Kierkegaard or a claim to 'justification by faith alone' must disprove what it attempts to proof. Natural theology is more balanced but its argument from analogy requires if not a 'leap of faith' too far but too greater a leap of logic.

Bibliography.

Bible (1962) Revised Standard Version, American Bible Society.

Chappell, T (2011) The Philosophy of Religion, Book 2, A222 Exploring Philosophy, Milton Keynes, The Open University.

Cornforth, M (1977) Materialism and the Dialectical Method, London, Lawrence and Wishart.

Cottingham, J (ed) (2008) Western Philosophy: An Anthology, Blackwell Publishing.

Davies, B (2004) An Introduction To The Philosophy Of Religion, New York, Oxford University Press.

Engels, F (1975) Ludwig Feuerbach and the End of Classical German Philosophy, Moscow, Progress Publishers.

Hume, D (2000) (ed) Tom.L.Beauchamp, An Enquiry concerning Human Understanding, New York, Oxford University Press.

Hume, D (1990 [1776]) Discourses concerning Natural Religion (ed Martin Bell), London, Penguin Classics

James, W (1902) The Varieties of Religious Experience, New York, Modern Library.

Marx, K (1975) Contribution to the Critique of Hegel's Philosophy of Law, Moscow, Progress Publishers.

Ree, J and Urmson, O.R (ed) (2005) The Concise Encyclopaedia of Western Philosophy, New York, Routledge.

Nietzsche, F (1977(1882)) A Nietzsche Reader, (ed) R.J.Hollingdale, London, Penguin Classics.

Sartre, J, P (1976) Being and Nothingness, London, Methuen & Co Ltd.

Sartre, J.P (1993) Essays in Existentialism, New York, Citadel Press.

Swinburne, R (1968) 'Miracles', Philosophy Quarterly. Philosophical Quarterly 18 (73).

According to Kuhn, what is wrong with Popper's account of the scientific method? Is Kuhn's criticism successful?

> Experiment escorts us last –
> His pungent company
> Will not allow an Axiom
> An Opportunity.
>> Dickenson, E (1975) p 715.

I would maintain that in order to explain Thomas Kuhn's critique of Karl Popper's account of the scientific method it is necessary to a) place Popper's account in the historical and theoretical context in which it occurred, b) delineate Popper's methodology in regard of the scientific method, c) outline Kuhn's perspective on the nature of scientific inquiry and d) assess Kuhn's criticism of Popper on scientific knowledge, e) evaluate to what extent that criticism is successful and finally f) to present my findings in regard of this philosophical discourse. Therefore my argument is that Karl Popper (1999 [1935]) The Logic of Scientific Discovery was responding to a tradition which found in Logical Positivism, during the 1920s and 1930s, a claim to have proved the 'verificationism' of scientific knowledge as attainable, an absolute 'Truth'. That as a result of this and Einstein's advances on Newton ideas Popper developed an alternative scientific method to the inductive and traditional model which can be derived from Francis Bacon where observations are generalized into theories. This mode of science relied on 'falsification' and 'demarcation criterion' between 'pseudo-science and science' and between 'dogmatic critical thinking'. This model then became dominant, a 'paradigm' and was challenged by Thomas Kuhn (1996 [1962]) The Structure of Scientific Revolutions in which he maintained that the practice of 'normal science' is both how science was practiced with the exception of 'scientific revolutions' is practiced and indeed provides the correct practice of science which has and does provide benefits for humanity. My argument will follow these parameters to conclude that the Emily Dickenson poem captures the essence of what science is, that is Kuhn's 'normal science'. I shall illustrate my position by arguing that Popper's position on astrology as 'pseudo-science' was correctly answered by Kuhn when he said that astrology was 'falsifiable' and therefore not 'pseudo-science' but by employing the concept of 'incommensurability' i.e. that two theories can only be judged by different benchmarks in the manner that Kuhn describes astrology is a 'craft' while he asserts correctly that medicine correctly is a 'science'.

Firstly, I will show that Popper can be seen as reacting against the Logical Positivists 'truth-claim' when as he states in Conjectures and

Refutations in (Cottingham 2011) p 454 'With Einstein's theory the situation was strikingly different':

These considerations lead me in the winter of 1919-1920 to conclusions which may be formulated as follows:

(1) It is easy to obtain confirmations, or verifications, for nearly every theory. – if we look for confirmations.

(2) Confirmation should count only if they are the result of risky predictions that is to say, if, unenlightened by the theory in question, we should have expected an event which was incompatible with the theory – an event which would have refuted the theory.

(3) Every 'good' scientific theory is a prohibition: it forbids certain thing.

(4) A theory which is not refutable by any conceivable event is non-scientific. Irrefutability is not a virtue of a theory…but a vice.

(5) Every genuine test of a theory is an attempt to refute it. Testability is flexibility; but there are degrees of testability: some theories are more testable, more exposed to refutation, than others; they take, as it were, greater risks.

(6) Confirming evidence should not count except when it is the result of a genuine test of the theory; and this means that it can be presented as a serious but unsuccessful attempt to falsify the theory…

(7) Some genuinely testable theories, when found to be false, are still found to be true, are still upheld by their admirers - for example by introducing ad hoc some auxiliary assumption.

Cottingham (2011) p 455.

Popper is advancing several concepts in regard of the scientific method here. He is making a claim for a 'demarcation criteria' between 'pseudo-science and science' and also describing his theory of 'falsification'. These two areas represent the major contributions that he made to the account of the scientific method. Therefore the differentiation between 'pseudo-science' and science and the necessity to falsify ideas as part of the methodology of science were for Popper inherent components of the scientific process. Popper's 'eureka moment' which Kuhn illustrates was in fact a moment derived from the long practice of' normal science', was not that Einstein disproved Newton theory itself, but rather that a model which was dominant, and appeared almost unassailable, had been disproved. Therefore falisability, the capacity for a scientific theory to be refutable in order for it to be proven was to become a central tenant of Popper scientific method. An example Popper uses is astrology in which he claims that 'confirmation data' is used to prevent 'falsification', in other words the astrologists can always add 'auxiliary information' to prove their claims are in some way correct. I shall consider Kuhn's response to this and its weight in regard scientific method further in my argument. To encapsulate Popper on the scientific method it is possible to say that he rejected empirical inductive method in favour of one based on deduction as employed in his method of conjectures and refutations whereby he creates a hypothesis and then 'severely' subject the hypothesis to tests in order to make a deductive inference. Essentially he has rejected induction and replaced it with a complexified deductive process. I have outlined Karl Popper's position on the scientific method both in terms of its historical context and that of its content.

To provide a description of Kuhn's criticism of Popper on the scientific method it is necessary to delineate the former's position.

For Kuhn science is a cycle which accumulates data and is characterized by long periods of 'normal science' which is science as understood a being science in the tradition which began with Bacon .This 'normal science' which Kuhn characterizes as 'problem solving' has brought humanity great benefits such as new medicines and the ability to travel to the moon. For Kuhn a scientific 'paradigm' is normally consistent and stable, it is only replaced when two factors become manifest 1) an 'accumulation of anomalies' within the present paradigm and 2) the existence of another improved 'paradigm with which to replace it'. In these conditions a 'scientific revolution' takes place and Kuhn draws parallels between these and the processes involved in political revolutions. Kuhn makes a point about the deferential relationship in the 'incommensurability' between pre-paradigmatic revolutionary 'crafts' and post-revolutionary 'science'. For Kuhn these cannot be measured by the same yardstick. To illustrate the Kuhn's point with a simple 'thought-experiment': cannot you measure Mozart and Motorhead, with the same yardstick because it is necessary and appropriate to apply different criteria or measurements as they existed in different periods and had different influences, they belong to different paradigms. The former may be the music of the spheres whilst the second is music to accompany amphetamine use, they cannot be measured by the same yardstick. In a similar way Kuhn argued that it is possible to separate astrology and astronomy, they are examples of a pre-scientific and post-scientific paradigm and 'the underdetermination of theory by data'.

What is wrong with Popper's account of the scientific method for Kuhn? Firstly, for the latter there are not spontaneous 'scientific revolutions' but they occur as the product of painstaking generations of 'normal science'. Popper places too much emphasis on the momentous transformations in science such as the movement from a Newtonian to an Einstein paradigm. This is a weakness in Popper's account of the scientific method; major scientific advances are not conjured up in the mind of a solitary genius but rather, following Kuhn, in the practice of 'normal science':

We should not lose sight of the fact that it took two hundred years of detailed work within the Newtonian paradigm and one hundred years of work within theories of electricity and magnetism to reveal the problems that Einstein was to recognize and solve with relativity.

Chalmers (2011) p 119-120.

Secondly, Popper would have to 'square the circle' in the sense that there cannot be another paradigm until one becomes available. If Copernicus had not provided an alternative heliocentric model of the universe to Ptolemy's geocentric one, there would not have been the paradigm available for Galileo to have made his advances.

Thirdly, the logic conclusion to Popper's theory of falsification is that there cannot be stable logic knowledge on which to found the scientific endeavour upon, for Popper there is falsification ad infinitum. Science needs a stable base of 'normal science' to make meaningful scientific progress. Thirdly for Kuhn the theory of scientific revolution represented the 'change' of a 'matrix of paradigms' for another and this is certainly a persuasive description of what happens when outsider scientists become mainstream . This is in contrast to Popper for falsification of one set of ideas and another arising out of it as a revolutionary process is not in the same sense. Fourthly, I would like to examine one of Popper's key claims i.e. the astrology is a 'pseudo-science', that it is therefore not falsifiable as it must be in order to be a science. Kuhn correctly directs us to 'collaborationism' here with pre and post-scientific paradigms. Popper is in making a 'valid' deductive argument in which he contradicts his overall position regarding the nature of the scientific method by 'denying the consequent' or mundus tollens. Therefore:

If p then q

Not q

Therefore not p

Premise I: If science is true then all astrological predictions must be proved to be wrong.

Premise 2 Not all astrological predictions are proved to be wrong.

Conclusion. Therefore not all science is true.

This is an inherent defect in Popper's own logic on scientific methodology. Kuhn is correct in arguing that falsification is possible in astrology and that scientific proof within a paradigm sometimes cannot be falsified, for example the human genotype DNA is beyond falsification within our present paradigm and there would have to be a 'scientific revolution' with a concomitant 'paradigm shift' to allow this. However I think it is important to keep in mind his differentiation between pre and post-revolutionary science as important here for Kuhn was clear about this demarcation and argues that astrology has the status of 'a craft' as opposed to medicine which is a 'science'. He is also correct in arguing that Popper's concept of the 'critical' discourse as defined as the rediscovery of the deductive tradition and inferring its empirical consequences is mistaken and in arguing:

'In a sense, to turn Sir Karl's view on its head, it is precisely the abandonment of critical discourse that marks the transition to science. Once a field has made that transition, critical discourse recurs only at moments of crisis when the bases of the field are again in jeopardy. Only when then must choose between competing theories do scientists behave like philosophers'

Kuhn (1970) pp. 6-9.

Kuhn's ability to contrast scientists with philosophers here is significant for philosophers ask the questions of epistemology and the philosophy of science while scientists practice it.

I would conclude that the Logical Positivists required to be answered theoretically but that Popper's theory of falsification denied science of its stable methodology, which is observation and experiments, until general patterns become apparent and then the formation of a hypothesis based on this process. I would agree with Kuhn (Ibid) that Popper's 'demarcation criterion...are impossible to support.' I maintain that Kuhn's criticism of Popper's account of the scientific method is cogent and the benefit of 'normal science' as a methodology within the tradition emanating from Bacon is apparent in the experience of humanity. I would agree with Emily Dickenson that indeed 'experiment' is the best 'escort' for human endeavour and that it proved itself to be so through the methodology of Inductivism which has been the paradigm of Western science since its Scientific Revolution.

Bibliography.

Chalmers, A.F (2011) What is this thing called Science? Maidenhead, The Open University Press.

Chimisso, C (2011) Knowledge Book 4 Open University Exploring Philosophy, Milton Keynes, The Open University.

Cottingham, J (ed) Western Philosophy: An Anthology, Oxford, Blackwell

Dickenson, E (1975) The Complete Poems, London, Faber and Fader.

Kuhn, T. S (1970) 'Logic of discovery of psychology of research? in Lakatos, I. and Musgrave, A. (eds) Criticism and the Growth of Knowledge, Cambridge, Cambridge University Press. pp. 6-9.

Kuhn, T.S (1996 [1962) The Structure of Scientific Revolutions, Chicago, University of Chicago Press.

Phelan, J.W (2005) Philosophy Themes and Thinkers. Cambridge, Cambridge University Press.

Popper, K (1999 [1935]) The Logic of Scientific Discovery, London, Routledge.

Popper, K (2002 [1963]) Conjectures and Refutations: The Growth of Scientific Knowledge, London, and Routledge.